MW00898511

THINGS FALL APART

by
Chinua Achebe

Teacher Guide

Written by
Mary L. Dennis

Note

The text used to prepare this guide was the Anchor Doubleday softcover, © 1959 by Chinua Achebe. The page references may differ in other editions.

Please note: Please assess the appropriateness of this book for the age level and maturity of your students prior to reading and discussing it with your class.

ISBN 1-56137-812-7

To order, contact your local school supply store, or—

Novel Units, Inc.
P.O. Box 433
Bulverde, TX 78163-0433

Web site: www.educyberstor.com

Table of Contents

Summary of *Things Fall Apart*

Things Fall Apart tells the story of Okonkwo, an Ibo tribesman living in the late 1800s in what is now Nigeria. After triumphing over his father's legacy of failure to become one of the most respected war heroes in his village, Okonkwo's stubborn pride in his reputation causes his eventual downfall. When British missionaries and government officials arrive to "civilize the savages," and clan members begin to abandon the old traditions of their barbaric religion in favor of Christianity and European-style commerce, Okonkwo is unable to adjust. While other clan leaders simply watch "things fall apart," Okonkwo makes one last bold move to rally a rebellion against the British intruders by beheading one of their court messengers with his machete. When none of his fellow clansmen follow his lead, Okonkwo hangs himself, a disgraceful act in the Ibo tradition. Untouchable by his own people, Okonkwo must be cut down and buried by the British. While his friends shake their heads in sad resignation, the District Commissioner muses that Okonkwo's story will make an interesting paragraph in the book the Commissioner is writing about his experiences among the savages.

About the Author

Born in 1930 in Ogidi, Eastern Nigeria, Chinua Achebe graduated from University College, Ibadan (now the University of Ibadan). He is one of Nigeria's most important writers. His novels analyze the effects of European colonization on Africa and particularly on the Ibo tribe of the southeastern portion of Nigeria.

Things Fall Apart (1958) tells of the arrival of European colonists and missionaries in the late 1800s. In subsequent novels, Achebe depicts the struggles of Africans to win back their independence. These novels include *No Longer At Ease* (1960)—considered a sequel to *Things Fall Apart*—*Arrow of God* (1964), *A Man of the People* (1966), and *Anthills of the Savannah* (1987).

Other writings include two volumes of poetry—*Beware, Soul Brother* and *Christmas in Biafra;* a collection of short stories—*Girls At War and Other Stories;* collected essays—*Hopes and Impediments* and *The Trouble with Nigeria;* and a children's book, *How the Leopard Got His Claws.*

Achebe has taught at the university level in Africa and in the United States, where he is now a professor at Bard College in New York. A recipient of numerous honors and awards, Achebe is a major contributor to world literature.

Background Information

During the Middle Ages, today's Federal Republic of Nigeria, a country located in western Africa on the Gulf of Guinea, was composed of organized kingdoms and states ruled by various ethnic groups. In the 17th and 18th centuries, slave traders from Portugal, England and other countries set up business in the delta area of the Niger river. Other Europeans explored along the river into the interior of the country. Before very long, the region was being exploited by Europeans for its abundant palm oil. British encroachment continued, and in 1914 the "Colony and Protectorate of Nigeria" was established. Nigerians were now officially under British rule.In the years following World War II, Nigerians began to demand independence from Britain. Through a series of constitutions which gradually yielded more power to the natives, Nigerian independence was finally granted in 1960.

Almost immediately, internal religious, political and ethnic problems led the new federation into civil war. Coups and counter-coups resulted in the deaths of many Africans. Members of the Ibo clan who had survived the slaughter returned to their homeland in eastern Nigeria and attempted to secede as their own nation, Biafra. This caused more civil strife, and the Biafran resistance effort was quelled.

Except for brief periods when the federation has operated as a democracy, Nigeria has been ruled by a military government since 1983. Plans for a transition to civilian government were negated in 1993 by a coup in November of that year in which General Sani Abacha became the Chief of State, Chief of Armed Forces, and Defense Minister. Since that coup, the Senate and House of Representatives have not met and most political parties have been outlawed.

Nigeria carries a large national debt and suffers from high unemployment and high inflation rates. It has increasingly become a trade route for cocaine coming from South America for distribution to European, Asian, and North American markets and for heroin coming from Asia and destined for Europe and North America.

Nigeria produces a great deal of the world's crude oil, and many Nigerians are concerned that the country's environment is being devastated by greedy military officials who cooperate with major oil companies. While those in power grow wealthy, many Nigerians remain poor and illiterate.

Major ethnic groups in Nigeria today are the Yoruba, the Ibo, the Hausa, and the Fulani. About 48% of Nigerians are Muslim, 34% are Christian, and 18% still practice traditional religions.

Initiating Activities

Choose one or more of the following prereading activities to help students draw from their background knowledge about the events and themes they will meet in *Things Fall Apart*.

1. **Anticipation Guide**

    Have students discuss whether they agree or disagree with the following statements—and why. (A more extensive reproducible version of this activity is included in the *Novel Units Student Packet* for this title.)

    a) A person's success can be judged by his or her material wealth.

    b) Ancestor worship is wrong.

    c) Every effort should be made to civilize primitive tribes and teach them Western ways.

    d) You should always respect your parents, even if you don't agree with the way they run their lives.

    f) A brave person does not always go along with the crowd.

2. **Viewing**

    a. *No Easy Walk*, a history of colonialism in Kenya, Zimbabwe, and Ethiopia; Cinema Guild.

    b. *Chinua Achebe*, 30 minutes, color; Films for the Humanities and Sciences, 800-257-5126.

    c. *Cry Freedom*, about the murder of Black Consciousness leader Steve Biko, who fought against apartheid in South Africa.

    d. *Out of Africa*, based on Isak Dinesen's book, while too long to be shown in its entirety, shows the beauty of African landscapes and the relationships between Europeans and natives.

3. **Reader Response Journal**

    In a three-column journal, students should note questions they have about (a) why Okonkwo or another character acts in a certain way; (b) why Achebe chose to include a particular proverb or story; (c) statements about their own feelings as they read the novel; (d) predictions they make about what will happen in the next chapter. Notes made in this journal can be used later in class discussion and in writing assignments.

4. **Pre-reading Discussion**

   About Superstition: What is superstition? What are some common examples? How and why do superstitions arise? Do you believe in any superstitions? Are superstitions part of organized religion—say, Catholicism? Judaism? Muslim? Buddhism? Do you believe in the power of dreams? Can dreams be a "sign"?

   About Africa: What do you know about the landscape, climate, and population of Africa? When the Europeans began to colonize this huge country, what effects were felt by the native population? What problems still exist today?

   About Culture Shock: What is culture shock? Have you ever experienced or witnessed being "torn between two cultures"? Are any young people in your community confronted by two cultures—the "American" culture at school, and another one at home? What conflicts does this create? How are students from different cultures treated at your school? Is there a respect for other cultures—or is there more often prejudice?

   About Folktales: What is a folktale? What elements do many folktales have in common? For example—what is the frog in a folktale usually like? How do you think folktales affect the lives of people who cannot read?

   About Proverbs: What is a proverb? Why does nearly every culture have its own proverbs? How seriously do most people take the advice contained in proverbs? Give an example of a proverb you feel is good advice. (example: "A stitch in time saves nine.") What do the following proverbs mean?
   - When the mouse laughs at the cat there is a hole nearby. *(Nigerian)*
   - If you can't bite, don't show your teeth. *(Yiddish)*
   - If fortune turns against you, even jelly breaks your tooth. *(Persian)*

5. **Role Play:** Have small groups of students improvise skits about the following situations (which are like situations in the story):

   a) Rather than getting a part-time job and studying to do well in school, a friend of yours spends all his time drinking, playing music, and partying with friends. Now he wants to borrow money from you—again.

   b) You're having trouble making a big decision. Your best friend suggests you call a psychic. The ads are on television all the time, and you've heard the call is free.

   c) You're helping a friend and his father do some work in the yard. The father is very dissatisfied with his son's work and begins berating and threatening him.

6. **Brainstorming:** Have students generate associations with a theme that is central to the story—such as SUCCESS, CHANGE or PRIDE while a student scribe jots ideas around the central word or statement on a large piece of paper or on an overhead transparency. Help students "cluster" the ideas into categories. A sample framework is shown below.

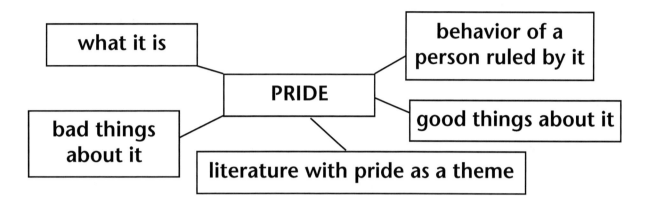

7. **Geography:** On a map, have students locate Nigeria, where the story takes place.

8. **Literary Analysis:** Have students read and discuss the lines by the Irish poet, W. B. Yeats, which precede Part One. This poem, "The Second Coming," was written in 1921 and expresses Yeats' concern over the rise of Fascism and what he saw as the disintegration of an old, safe way of life. Yeats used the term "gyre" to refer to a cycle of history. The entire poem is only 22 lines and can be the basis of a class discussion about how our own civilization seems at times to be "falling apart."

    You might extend this activity by asking students to bring in newspaper or magazine articles describing events they feel are representative of a society (our own or a foreign one) in which "the center cannot hold."

9. **Writing:** Have students freewrite in their literature journals, using these sentence starters:

    When a man shows weakness …
    A thinking man …
    A man of action …
    Primitive tribes …
    Religious custom …

Some Ideas for Vocabulary Study

Ibo Words

There are many Ibo words in *Things Fall Apart* which will be unfamiliar to students. The "Glossary of Ibo Words and Phrases" on pages 211-212 is helpful, and some of the words can be defined from context. To avoid constant flipping back and forth, have the students skim the assigned chapters for Ibo words (they will be italicized), look them up in the glossary, and use small sticky notes to attach the definitions to the relevant pages.

Other Vocabulary Activities

1. Have the students map words, including several synonyms, an antonym if appropriate, some other forms of the word, a memory device or sketch to help them recall the definition, and/or some way to associate the word with their own experiences. The format can be left up to the students, or use a framework like the one below.

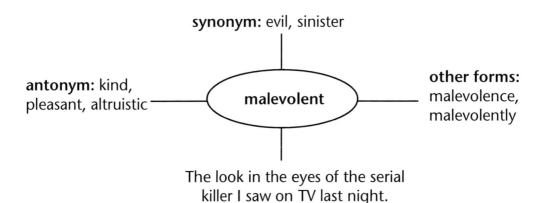

synonym: evil, sinister

antonym: kind, pleasant, altruistic — **malevolent** — other forms: malevolence, malevolently

The look in the eyes of the serial killer I saw on TV last night.

For a vocabulary list with many entries, make each student responsible for just one or two words. Display the maps and give students ample opportunity to view them and make their own notes about words with which they are not familiar.

2. Have the students create analogies for the words, using as many specific vocabulary words as possible in each analogy. For example, an analogy for the list for Chapters 1-3 could read "**Sinister : malevolent :: impending : approaching**," using three list words in one analogy.

3. Have the students compose questions to ask classmates about the words. For example, a student might ask "When can **kites** fly by themselves?" The correct answer would be something like, "When the kites are a species of bird."

4. Divide the class into pairs and assign several words to each pair. After arriving at a simple definition for each of their assigned words, partners should create a mnemonic device to help them remember the definition. Definitions and mnemonics can be shared with the class.

5. Investigate the etymology of words on the list. Make semantic maps showing the root words and meanings and some other forms of the word.

6. Challenge students to use as many list words as possible in the same sentence. It is permissible to use varying forms of the words. Provide an incentive for the winner. The sentences can be a bit ridiculous, but should still use the words properly and make sense. An example for the word list for Chapters 10-13: "He could **discern** the **notorious** sacred birds displaying their **plumage** and making their **vigorous, eloquent** sounds, and he thought with **profound approbation** that in spite of the **tumult** and **pandemonium** it would cause in the village if he '**inadvertently**' killed one, it would almost be worth it to taste the **delectable** flesh."

7. At the beginning of your study of *Things Fall Apart*, have students make separate pages in their notebooks with the headings "Emotion Describers;" "Place or Thing Describers;" "Sensory Describers" (sound, taste, smell); "People Describers." As students proceed with the reading, have them add words to the pages.

8. Have students use a prescribed number of the vocabulary words in a poem with a specific form, such as a Cinquain, Limerick, Diamante, Haiku, or Sonnet.

9. Before they read a section, have students predict how the words on the vocabulary list will be used. For example, in Chapters 7-9—Who will be *rebuked?* Will the *entrails* be human or animal? What event might be connected with an *emissary?*

Discussion Questions • Vocabulary
Writing Ideas • Activities

Chapters 1-3, pp. 7-27

Summary: Okonkwo, an Ibo tribesman living in the nine-village area of Africa known as Umuofia, has worked very hard to become a success, but he is still dominated by his fear of becoming like his failed father and often treats people harshly. Ikemefuna, a boy from Mbaino, was given to Umuofia as a peace offering, and is being raised by one of Okonkwo's three wives.

Vocabulary

harmattan 3	improvident 4	cowries 4	haggard 4
kites 5	kola nut 6	ancestral 6	impending 6
plaintive 6	proverbs 7	prowess 8	revered 8
overtone 9	sinister 9	uncanny 9	vibrant 10
trill 10	orator 10	ultimatum 11	imperious 12
emissary 12	capricious 13	malevolent 13	incipient 13
prosperity 14	priestess 16	machete 17	abomination 18
contemptible 18	sisal 23	luxuriant 24	inflexible 24

Discussion Questions

1. How did Okonkwo become famous even beyond the nine villages of Umuofia? *(He threw the wrestler, Amalinze.)* What do you think their fight was like? Do "good fighters" in your neighborhood enjoy any special treatment or privileges? Why do you suppose Okonkwo's neighbors and family put up with his fiery temper?

2. What words does Achebe use to describe Unoka? *(improvident, haggard, a debtor, mournful, a failure, a loafer)* What made Unoka happy? *(He liked to drink, play music, have his friends around.)* Do people who party too much and who don't repay their debts usually end up as Unoka did?

3. What do Unoka and Okoye have in common? In what ways are they different? *(Use a graphic like the following on the board or overhead.)*

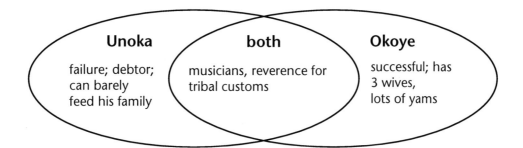

Unoka
failure; debtor; can barely feed his family

both
musicians, reverence for tribal customs

Okoye
successful; has 3 wives, lots of yams

4. Why did Okoye come to see Unoka? *(He wanted him to repay a debt of 200 cowries.)* Why did Unoka say, "…the sun will shine on those who stand before it shines on those who kneel under them"? *(He was telling Okoye he considered his big debts more important than this small one to Okoye.)* Do you think Okoye was angry with Unoka?

5. How was Okonkwo able to become wealthy and famous when his father owed so much to everyone? *(Each man is judged an as individual, on the basis of his own achievements.)*

6. Judging from the last few sentences of Chapter 1, how important do you think Ikemefuna will be in this story? What do the words "doomed" and "ill-fated" tell you?

7. How do you feel about Okonkwo's war triumphs—and his "wineglass" for special occasions? Do you think he would have minded being sent off to war again? Do most soldiers have no fear of war?

8. What important news does Ogbuefi Ezeugo bring the 10,000 men in the marketplace—and what action is taken? *(Ezeugo explains that an Umuofian woman has been murdered by someone in Mbaino. Mbaino was given a choice of going to war or giving up a young man and woman. The latter option was chosen, and Okonkwo went to Mbaino to get the boy and girl.)*

9. What magical source of "war medicine" makes other clans fear the power of Umuofia? *(The source is an old woman with one leg.)* Who does Umuofia always consult before deciding to wage war? *(the Oracle of the Hills and Caves)*

10. What happened to the girl from Mbaino? *(She was given to Ogbuefi Udo to replace his murdered wife.)* Do you suppose Udo was satisfied with the "replacement"? How do you imagine the girl feels? What happened to the boy, Ikemefuna? *(He was sent to live with Okonkwo's family.)* How does he feel about his new home? *(He is afraid, confused, lonely.)*

11. What was the Oracle's explanation for Unoka's failing crops? *(The priestess, who interpreted Agbala's messages, said that Unoka was physically weak and lazy.)* How did his "bad chi" follow him to his death? *(He became ill with swelling and was taken to the Evil Forest to die alone.)* What do you imagine his final days were like?

12. What is Okonkwo's greatest fear? *(that he will be like his father)* He tells Nwakibie he is different from other young men. How? *(Okonkwo says he is not afraid of hard work.)* What does Nwakibie get in return for giving Okonkwo the seed yams? *(two-thirds of the harvest)*

13. How do drought and flood in our country affect farmers? consumers? What help is available? How did Okonkwo find a positive side to the sad harvest? *(He knew if he could survive that year, he could survive anything.)*

    Prediction: Will Ikemefuna be treated as a son or as a slave by Okonkwo and his family?

Supplementary Activities

Author's Craft

Achebe tells us that members of the clan often talk in **proverbs**, "the palm oil with which words are eaten."

Ask: What does this metaphor about proverbs tell you about the **reason** the Ibo use them? (It is easier to say something difficult or unpleasant by using a proverb, which allows you to say it indirectly.)

Have students find and analyze examples of proverbs in Chapters 1-3. (e.g., page 6, "He who brings kola brings life;" page 8, "If a child washed his hands he could eat with kings;" page 10, "When the moon is shining the cripple becomes hungry for a walk;" page 19, "A man who pays respect to the great paves the way for his own greatness.")

Writing Activities

1. Choose a proverb you've heard your "elders" use. Identify a situation involving you in which they might use the proverb. Explain the "message" behind the proverb.

2. Unoka makes a distinction between *general* and *individual* failure. Give an example of each type in your world. Do you agree with Unoka that general failure is easier to survive? Why or why not?

Research

"Yam, the king of crops, was a man's crop" (page 23). Find out more about the type of yams grown in Africa. How are they like/unlike the sweet potatoes and yams grown in the United States? What are some good reasons for eating yams? What are some ways to prepare them?

Chapters 4-6, pp. 28-56

Summary: Ikemefuna begins to feel like part of Okonkwo's family. Okonkwo is punished by the earth goddess for beating one of his wives during the Week of Peace. Okonkwo berates his gentle son, Nwoye, for the way he cuts yams for planting, and shoots his gun at Ekwefi, his second wife, whom he has just beaten for cutting some leaves from a banana tree. There is a feast and a wrestling match.

Vocabulary

brusqueness 26	contradicted 26	kindred 26	communal 28
plait 29	ordained 30	repentant 31	valediction 32
disquieting 33	dynamism 34	arduous 34	calabashes 36
reveled 38	tentative 38	pottage 43	grandees 46
bouts 47	disembodied 50		

Discussion Questions

1. What did the oldest man at the kindred meeting mean when he said "those whose palm kernels were cracked for them by a benevolent spirit should not forget to be humble"? *(He meant that Okonkwo happened to have good luck and success, but that didn't give him the right to act superior.)* Do you think Okonkwo was "just lucky"? *(He had worked hard to overcome his misfortune.)* How did Okonkwo use "the power of positive thinking"? *(He said "yes" and his chi said yes; i. e., he believed in himself.)*

2. How did Ikemefuna adjust to his new home? *(He was fearful and homesick at first, but Nwoye and Nwoye's mother were kind and this helped him.)* How did Okonkwo treat Ikemefuna? *(He treated him "with a heavy hand" but was inwardly fond of him.)* Do you think Ikemefuna could tell that Okonkwo really liked him?

3. How did Okonkwo get in trouble with Ezeani? *(Okonkwo beat one of his wives, Ojiugo, during the Week of Peace, when it was unheard of to beat anyone.)* Do

you think he was punished mostly because he hurt his wife or mostly because he disrespected the gods and ancestors? *(The priest agrees the wife was at fault; apparently wife-beating would be quite acceptable during a different week.)*

4. How did Okonkwo's evil act affect his reputation in the village? *(People said he had gone too far, that his good fortune had gone to his head.)* Do you think they were secretly glad he had done something wrong?

5. Why does Okonkwo threaten to break Nwoye's jaw, strangle him, break his head? *(He is not satisfied with the way Nwoye prepares the seed yams.)* Do you think being such a threatening, pushy parent will make Nwoye turn out as Okonkwo hopes?

6. To which U. S. holiday could you compare the Feast of the New Yam? *(Thanksgiving, Kwaanza, New Year's Day)* Why do you suppose food is so often a part of religious and holiday celebrations of all kinds, everywhere?

7. Do you find any irony in Okonkwo's prayers to his ancestors (page 39) to "protect him, his children, and their mothers"? *(He has just beaten and shot at one wife. He treats everyone harshly.)*

8. On pages 40-41, what evidence do you see that the Ibo peoples' lives are controlled by superstition? *(Ezinma's twitching eyelid "means she will see something;" Ekwefi doesn't answer "yes" for fear there will be an evil spirit at the door.)*

9. What are the tasks of the women and girls in the village? *(They do the cooking, weed the gardens, plant crops like melons and beans.)* Do you think they are happy with their lives? Do you suppose all fathers in the village treat their little girls as Okonkwo treats Ezinma and Obiageli—or are some more affectionate?

10. Why does Ekwefi tell Chielo, "I cannot find a mouth with which to tell the story" (page 48)? *(She still can't believe Okonkwo shot at her.)* Why does Chielo say she thinks Ezinma will "stay"? Where would she go? *(She means that Ezinma has passed through the ages when childhood illness might have killed her—she's now likely to "stay" in the land of the living.)* How do you know Ezinma means everything to her mother? *(Ekwefi sighs, "I pray she stays," page 48.)* Is the priestess of Agbala as you expected?

11. What were the most exciting moments in the wrestling matches? *(when a man was thrown)* How do you think these matches were like/unlike those televised today, for example the World Wrestling Federation matches?

    Prediction: Why will the villagers of Umuofia be delighted with an invasion of locusts?

Supplementary Activities

Literary Analysis: Point of View

Point of view refers to the vantage point from which the narrator views the action of the story and relates it to the reader. In a **first-person** narrative, the story is told from the viewpoint of one person, usually the main character. A **third-person omniscient** narrator can "see over" everything that is happening and into each character's heart and mind. A **third-person limited** point of view means there are some restrictions on what can be seen; the narrator may know only what is happening to a few characters in one setting.

Ask: From what point of view does Achebe tell the story in *Things Fall Apart?* (third person omniscient) How do you know? (We are told about the inner feelings of many of the characters; Achebe "sees" what is happening all over the village.)

Writing Activities

1. Reread the description of the conversation between Ekwefi and Chielo on pages 48-49. Rewrite the scene from the first-person point of view ("I..."). Choose either Ekwefi or Chielo as your narrator.

2. Write a character sketch of someone you know who likes to act superior to others and puts down those who are less successful. (Be sure to give the person a fictitious name.) You might first organize your thoughts by jotting character traits and examples in a graphic like the one below.

3. Write the letter Ikemefuna might send to his mother during his first days at Umuofia.

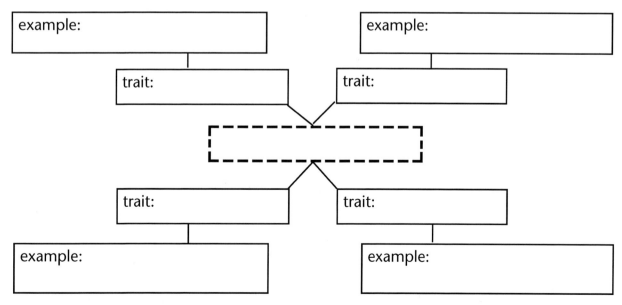

Chapters 7-9, pp. 51-82

Summary: The people welcome a locust invasion, roasting and eating the insects. Ikemefuna had lived in Okonkwo's household for three years and was treated like a son, yet when the elders decided he must be killed, Okonkwo participated, against the advice of Ogbuefi Ezeudu. Nwoye's feelings about his father and tribal custom begin to change. We learn that Ezinma is the only one of ten children borne by Ekwefi who has lived. When she becomes ill, the medicine man is called in to help locate and dig up an evil rock which it is believed may cause Ezinma's death. Okonkwo cannot hide his concern about Ezinma, who he says "should have been a boy."

Vocabulary

feign 52	espied 54	entrails 54	rebuked 54
harbingers 56	copiously 56	pestle 58	effeminate 58
plantains 63	valor 65	coiffure 71	audacity 76
resignation 77	devoid 77	defiant 77	specious 80
manifest 81			

Discussion Questions

1. Why did Okonkwo tell the boys stories of violence and bloodshed? *(This was supposed to make them more masculine, more inclined to violence themselves.)* What movies do you think Okonkwo would rent from the video store if he were around today? Which movies would Nwoye choose?

2. In the 1800s, invasions of locusts devastated crops in the American midwest and left farmers in financial ruin. How does the attitude of the Ibo people toward locusts compare to that of American farmers? *(The Ibo are overjoyed to see them coming.)* What do they do with the locusts? *(They are caught, roasted, dried and eaten as a delicacy.)*

3. What was your initial reaction to Ezeudu's statement, "Umuofia has decided to kill him" (page 57)? Do you think Nwoye's mother had any idea what was planned for Ikemefuna?

4. How was it possible for Okonkwo to kill Ikemefuna, who thought of Okonkwo as his real father? *(Okonkwo was "afraid of being thought weak.")* Do you think his action is justifiable in any way? What do you wish he had done?

5. Nwoye felt something inside him give way when he realized Ikemefuna had been killed. What other time had he felt this way? *(when he heard an infant crying in the forest and realized it was one of twins who had been "thrown away")* Do you think Nwoye will continue to try to please his father?

6. What seems to bother Okonkwo most about Ikemefuna's death? *(He is bothered by his own inability to casually pass off the killing of a boy.)* Why do you think he says of Ezinma, "She should have been a boy" (page 64)?

7. What is your opinion of Obierika's advice to Okonkwo regarding what he should have done on the day he killed Ikemefuna (page 67)?

8. Why do you think Achebe included the story about Ndulue and Ozoemena? *(Perhaps he was trying to show that Ndulue, unlike Okonkwo, was not afraid to show feelings for his wife. He knew he would still be respected as a brave warrior.)*

9. From the description of Akueke on page 73 and the description of the haggling over her bride-price, what can you conclude about the Ibo's opinion of women? *(They seem to be valued for their physical beauty and fertility, but might be considered property by our standards.)*

10. Why is Ezinma's illness so upsetting to Ekwefi? *(Of the ten children she bore, Ezinma is the only one to live past the age of three. Naturally, Ekwefi has always been anxious about Ezinma's health.)*

11. Describe the belief regarding the *obanje* and the *iyi-uwa*. *(An obanje is a child who repeatedly dies and is reborn; the iyi-uwa, a special stone forming the link between the obanje and the spirit world, must be destroyed to keep the child alive.)*

12. Do you think Ezinma really buried the *iyi-uwa* under the orange tree—or was it just coincidence that the medicine man found a stone wrapped in a rag in the place where Ezinma told him to dig? How else might such a stone have gotten there?

13. Did Okonkwo act "in character"—as you know him so far—when Ezinma became ill? *(This is the only time we have seen him show real concern for anyone.)* To what do you attribute his behavior?

Prediction: What will happen to Ezinma next?

Supplementary Activities

Author's Craft: Irony

Achebe often uses **irony**, a mildly humorous way of presenting a discrepancy between what is said and what the author really means. **Ask:** What is ironic about Obierika's reference to Abame and Aninta (page 73)? *(He complains that women are haggled over like property—yet the Umuofians aren't much better.)*

Writing Activity

Nwoye prefers his mother's stories to the violent ones Okonkwo tells. Think about the stories you loved as a child and the kind you prefer now. How are they alike? How are they different? Write a comparison-and-contrast essay.

Research/Speaking Activity

Folktales are an important part of many cultures. Read some African folktales, and choose one to tell to your classmates. You don't have to memorize the folktale word-for-word—just tell the story in your own words. (A good source: *World Folktales* by Atelia Clarkson and Gilbert B. Cross, Scribner, 1980/1984.)

Chapters 10-13, pp. 83-112

Summary: A domestic dispute is settled in a public ceremony. The priestess, Chielo, takes Ezinma to the cave of Agbala, the oracle. Her nervous parents follow in the darkness, and we see a human side of Okonkwo. There is a pre-wedding ceremony for Obierika's daughter. Ezeudu dies, and at his funeral Okonkwo's gun explodes and kills one of Ezeudu's sons. Okonkwo and his family are banished from Umuofia for seven years.

Vocabulary

guttural 88	pandemonium 88	esoteric 88	raffia 89
approbation 91	impenetrably 95	notorious 95	voluble 97
plumage 97	eloquent 98	delectable 98	prophesy 100
profound 104	vigor 104	discern 106	benumbed 107
tripods 112	mortars 113	sediment 120	tremulous 121
unearthly 121	tumult 122	inadvertent 124	

Discussion Questions

1. What are the *egwugwu? (men dressed to represent the spirits of ancestors)* Why are there nine? *(Each represents a village of Umuofia.)* How do you think the *egwugwu* named Evil Forest got the smoke to pour from his head?

2.   What is the purpose of the gathering at the *ilo*? *(Uzowulu is protesting that his brothers-in-law took back his wife, Mgbafo, and their children. Odukwe, Mgbafo's brother, claims they had to rescue their sister from daily beatings.)* Do you think Mgbafo returned to Uzowulu?

3.   Do you think Ekwefi's story about the tortoise has any parallels with the story you're reading? Is Tortoise anything like Okonkwo?

4.   Why do you think Chielo came to get Ezinma? What do you imagine Okonkwo thought when Ekwefi said she was going to follow Chielo?

5.   As Ekwefi waits outside the ring of hills for Chielo to bring Ezinma out, who suddenly appears? *(Okonkwo)* Were you surprised? How is the tone of the last paragraph of Chapter 11 different from any we have seen so far? *(For once Okonkwo shows a little concern for Ekwefi, telling her to go home and sleep; she remembers their early "courtship.")*

6.   To what might you compare the *uri* for Obierika's daughter? *(It is something like an engagement party or wedding shower.)*

7.   How does the *ekwe* serve as a sort of public-address system? *(It broadcasts the news of Ezeudu's death.)* To what might you compare its language of rhythmic sounds for communication? *(Morse code, for example)* Why does the news make Okonkwo nervous? *(Ezeudu had warned him to bear no hand in Ikemefuna's death.)*

8.   How do you suppose the "most dreaded" *egwugwu* got flies to follow him?

9.   Compare a typical funeral for a military hero in the United States with the funeral for Ezeudu. Use a graphic like the one below.

U. S. Military Hero	Ezeudu
sombre music and behavior	frenzied activity
singing patriotic songs, hymns	dancing and singing
firing guns and cannon	firing guns and cannon
airplane salutes	killing animals and trees
riderless horse	appearance of *egwugwu*
dark clothing	painted bodies

10. Do you see any ironic connection between Ezeudu's warning to Okonkwo and Okonkwo's crime? *(Ezeudu told Okonkwo not to kill Ikemefuna; Okonkwo intentionally did so but was not punished. When Okonkwo accidentally killed Ezeudu's son, he lost everything.)*

11. How did Obierika justify destroying Okonkwo's living quarters, animals and barn? *(The land had to be cleansed; the earth goddess had to be satisfied.)* Did he have any second thoughts about this kind of "justice"? *(Yes; he realized it seemed unfair, just as it had seemed unfair to him to "throw away" his twin infants. He accepted the customs, however.)*

Prediction: How will Okonkwo and his family be treated in Mbanta?

Supplementary Activities

Literary Analysis: Simile

A **simile** is a figure of speech used to compare two unlike things to create a "mental picture" for the reader. For example, "Okonkwo was as slippery as a fish in water" (page 3). Have students identify other examples of similes in Part One. [An example from this reading section: "…settled like a sediment of sorrow on the earth" (p. 120).]

Writing Activities

1. After Okonkwo left for Mbanta, his friends destroyed his property. In their society, have they committed any crime? In our society, would they be criminals? Defend your answer.

2. Rap is a rhythmic way of communicating, just as the drums in Umuofia communicated important messages to the people. Write a short rap about Okonkwo. Think about the major events in his life so far (through Part One) and describe them, or assume the persona of another character in the story—Ekwefi or Obierika, for instance—and put in your rap the things you imagine they would like to say to or about Okonkwo.

Part Two

Chapters 14-16, pp. 119-137

Summary: Uchendu, Okonkwo's uncle on his mother's side, welcomes Okonkwo and his three wives and children to Mbanta. They help him make a home there and plant a new farm, but Okonkwo is in the depths of despair. Obierika comes to visit, and brings news of white men destroying the village of Abame. In a few years, missionaries build a church in Umuofia, and Nwoye joins them. They have come to Mbanta, too, but after listening to an evangelist explain Christianity, Okonkwo is sure the man is crazy and that no one will take him seriously.

Vocabulary

refuge 119	requisite 129	affirmation 131	mirthless 134
woeful 138	albino 138	audibly 140	ominous 140
evangelists 143	dialect 144	heathen 145	derisive 146
rollicking 146	enthralled 146	captivated 147	marrow 147
callow 147			

Discussion Questions

1. Uchendu and his sons are generous and helpful to Okonkwo. If he had committed an intentional—"male"—crime, might they have acted differently? What if they knew about Ikemefuna?

2. What are "the nuts of the water of heaven"? *(hailstones)* How do you think the residents of Mbanta would react to snow?

3. Why is Okonkwo so depressed? *(He has been cast out by his clan, feels too tired and old to start over, and is disappointed that his personal god keeps saying "no.")*

4. In Chapter 12, Akeuke went to live with her suitor's family for seven weeks. At what point in the series of ceremonies are Amikwu and his bride-to-be? *(last)*

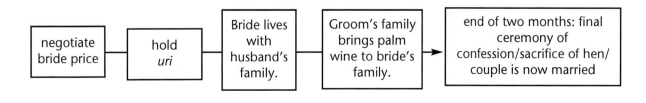

5. What do you think is the purpose of the family meeting called by Uchendu, pages 133-135? *(He is telling Okonkwo not to feel so sorry for himself, to stop being so macho and to value his mother's kinsmen and his own wives and children.)* Is Uchendu a "thinking man" like Obierika or a "man of action" like Okonkwo? *(Uchendu seems to be a deep thinker.)*

6. What frightening news about Abame does Obierika bring? *(A white man "riding an iron horse" had appeared in Abame and was killed on the advice of the Oracle. Later, on market day, other whites and natives from another village killed almost everyone.)* What do you think the "iron horse" was? *(a bicycle)*

7. Why does Uchendu tell the story about the kite? *(It reminds the others that it wasn't wise to kill a man who didn't speak.)* Do you think that, like in the folk tale, "there is something ominous behind the silence" in this tale of the white men in Abame?

8. Is Obierika serious when he tells Okonkwo he could thank him by killing one of his sons—or himself? *(This seems to be a joke.)*

9. The white missionary spoke through an Ibo interpreter. What was funny about this? *(The interpreter's dialect was different from that spoken in Mbanta, and when he meant "myself" he said "my buttocks." A joker in the crowd made the most of the opportunity to get some laughs.)* How is this another example of irony? *(Books and movies of the "civilized" world make fun of the natives' language, which they portray as little more than grunts and whoops. Here the situation is reversed.)*

10. Why did Nwoye tell Obierika that Okonkwo is not his father? *(Nwoye liked what the missionaries said about the Christian religion. Perhaps he doesn't feel the need of harsh Okonkwo now that he has a kindly heavenly father.)*

   Prediction: What effects do you think the arrival of the missionaries will have on the future lives of Okonkwo, his wives, and his children?

Supplementary Activities

Writing Activity
Amikwu's young bride answers the confession question knowing that if she lies she will suffer and possibly die in childbirth. Isn't it possible she could suffer and die anyway—and if she does, won't people say she lied at the confession? Write an interior monologue for the young bride the night before the confession ceremony as she thinks about this no-win situation.

Chapters 17-19, pp. 138-156

Summary: To the Mbanta rulers' amazement, the missionaries gratefully accept a piece of land in the "evil forest" for their church. Soon some of the village people become converts, impressed by the power of the "white man's fetish" to survive in the sinister place. After a beating by Okonkwo, Nwoye joins the missionaries for good. The number of converts grows to a small community, ostracized by the non-Christians. As Okonkwo's seven years of exile in Mbanta draw to a close, he celebrates with a big feast. One of the tribal elders reminds the young people of the importance of keeping the clan together, of speaking with one voice. He warns them of his fears that the white man's church will destroy tribal kinship.

Vocabulary

gospel 148	persevered 148	fetishes 148	dispersed 149
impudent 150	unduly 151	perturbed 151	forsake 152
miscreant 152	despicable 152	enormity 152	annihilation 153
degenerate 153	impotent 154	outcasts 155	derision 156
taboo 156	caste 156	adherents 157	zeal 157
python 157	emanation 157	atonement 158	blasphemous 158
ostracize 159	debar 160		

Discussion Questions

1. Why did Uchendu offer the missionaries land in the Evil forest? *(He thought they'd refuse it.)* Once the land was accepted and the building began, what did the people of Mbanta expect would happen? *(They thought the missionaries would be killed by the evil spirits.)* How did Uchendu's plan backfire? *(The people were impressed by the white men's apparent power over death, and converts were won.)*

2. Do you think Okonkwo would have really killed Nwoye if Uchendu hadn't stopped him? What did Okonkwo decide about Nwoye as he looked at the fire? *("Living fire begets cold, impotent ash;" e.g., Okonkwo=a flaming fire=success; Nwoye=cold ash=failure.)*

3. Why do you think Mr. Kiaga told Nwoye, "Blessed is he who forsakes his father and his mother for my sake" (page 152)? Do you think he was within his rights to encourage Nwoye to forget about his parents—or had Nwoye already decided for himself anyway? *(Nwoye finds it a relief to leave his father for good; he hopes to convert his mother and siblings later on.)*

4. At first, why didn't the clan worry much about the new church? *(They thought those who became converts were worthless anyway, no loss to the clan.)*

5. What were some incidents that caused problems between the church and the clan? What were the eventual outcomes?

Incident	Problem	Outcome
Converts declared clan's gods dead and powerless, threatened to burn shrines.	Clan members insulted and beat converts.	no further problems for some time
Okoli killed the sacred python, according to the Christians.	Church converts were ostracized; Okoli died.	Clan saw Okoli's death as proof of their gods' powers.

6. How was Mr. Kiaga able to keep the church from foundering when it began admitting *osu*—outcasts? *(He explained that everyone is a child of God, that the osu needed Christ more than anyone. When the converts still doubted, Mr. Kiaga's own firm faith finally convinced them.)* Do you think the converts finally consciously realized that it wasn't humanly "right" to cast out certain people—or did they simply accept the situation "on faith"? What is the difference in the two ways of reacting?

7. What would Okonkwo really enjoy doing regarding the church? *(He'd like to chase all the Christians out of the village with whips.)* Does Okonkwo's reaction to the church seem typical of the way he reacts to most things? *(He usually thinks of violent solutions to problems.)*

    Prediction: One of the tribal elders at the feast voices his fears about the future and the effects he fears the "abominable religion" will have. What could this possibly foreshadow about Okonkwo's return to Umuofia?

Supplementary Activities

Writing Activity
Uchendu says "...he that has health and children will also have wealth." What kind of "wealth" is he talking about? Do you agree with him? Explain your answer

Literary Analysis: Indirect Characterization
Indirect Characterization is a subtle way of telling us about a character. Achebe doesn't waste words describing Mr. Kiaga directly, yet he is quite important to the plot and to the "social milieu" of Mbanta in this section. What can you infer about Mr. Kiaga through Achebe's indirect characterization techniques? What details have you supplied from your own imagination?

Part Three

Chapters 20-22, pp. 157-175

Summary: Although Okonkwo has lost his place of importance in Umuofia, he is determined to regain prestige through his remaining five sons and by marrying off his daughters to important Umuofians. In Umuofia, there is now a "white man's government" which judges natives by its own laws. The government employs a number of native court messengers, who are hated for their arrogance and complicity with the whites. Mr. Brown, the white missionary, treats the villagers with respect, encourages them to send their children to his school and has built a small hospital. It soon becomes evident that those who go to school can get good jobs with the white government and earn money to trade for goods at the stores. Mr. Brown is replaced by Mr. Smith, an uncompromising zealot who instigates so much enmity between the church and the clan that his church is finally burned to the ground.

Vocabulary

irreparable 171	esteem 172	resilient 171	buoyant 173
indignity 175	dispensation 178	lunatic 178	expedient 178
singlets 181	accommodation 184	tares 184	idolatrous 184
deterred 185	desecrated 186	amulets 187	parsonage 188
imminent 188	discordant 188	composure 189	pacified 191

Discussion Questions

1. What does Achebe mean by "the tragedy of his [Okonkwo's] first son"? *(Nwoye's conversion to Christianity)* What dreams does Okonkwo have for his remaining five sons? *(that they will be titled, successful)*

2. Who is clearly Okonkwo's favorite child? *(Ezinma)* Does it surprise you that she can have such sympathy for her father when he is so harsh? What plans does Okonkwo have for Ezinma and Obiageli? *(that they will marry important men in Umuofia and add to Okonkwo's prestige)*

3. What have the white men brought to Umuofia in addition to the church? *(a system of government that judges Umuofians according to white law and punishes them with imprisonment, hard labor, hanging)* How would you react if you were an Umuofian imprisoned for doing something your clan has done for centuries—for example, for "throwing away" twins? How do you think the British justified judging others by their own laws?

4. According to Obierika, how have have the whites "put a knife on the things that held us together" (page 176)? *(Many Ibo have joined the white man's way of life; the clan has lost its unity; "things fall apart.")* In what circumstances might you feel as Obierika feels?

5. How was Mr. Brown able to win the respect of so many people in Umuofia? *(He avoided angering the clan, talked with the leaders about religion, and built a school and hospital.)* Do you think he caused any harm in the community?

6. Important political issues in the United States are education, jobs, and the economy. What evidence is there that these are now becoming important issues in Umuofia? *(Those who attend school can get government jobs which provide them with money to spend at the trading store, where palm oil and kernel now bring a large profit and improve the area's economy.)*

7. Compare Mr. Brown's religion with the Ibo religion.

Mr. Brown's Christianity	Ibo religion
one loving God	fearsome supreme god (Chukwu)
God is head of church	and many lesser gods
God is all-powerful	idol-worship
	gods seen as people
	ancestor worship

8. Were Okonkwo's seven years of planning his return a waste of time? *(The people are more interested in the church, government jobs and stores than they are in the return of Okonkwo. The old ways of the clan are giving way to change.)* What is at stake for Okonkwo—and why is it particularly important to him to maintain the old ways? *(His hopes for his sons and daughters are all grounded in the old traditions of the village. He could take no pride in a child who becomes a Christian or goes to school.)*

9. How does Reverend Smith compare with Mr. Brown? *(He is an uncompromising zealot and probably a racist; he sees the Ibo as totally evil and himself and his church as totally good.)* How does Reverend Smith prove the clan's saying, "...that as a man danced so the drums were beaten for him" (page 185)? *(Reverend Smith's zeal stirred Enoch to unmask an egwugwu, and this eventually led to the church being burned down.)*

10. Explain the line on page 187, "It seemed as if the very soul of the tribe wept for a great evil that was coming—its own death." *(Enoch's unthinkable action is like a harbinger of what is yet to come.)*

    Prediction: "...for the moment the spirit of the clan was pacified" (page 191): How long will it be before there is more trouble?

Supplementary Activities

Writing Activities

1. Ajofin says, "We say he is foolish because he does not know our ways, and perhaps he says we are foolish because we do not know his." Think about some contemporary conflicts in terms of Ajofin's statement: for example, the conservative-versus-liberal controversy, racial problems, religious differences, the "war between the sexes." Using one of these topics, or another of your own choosing, write a short essay in which you try to help someone "on the other side of the issue" to better understand your side's viewpoint.

2. Ezinma and Okonkwo have a special understanding, while Okonkwo and Nwoye are no longer even speaking. With a partner, make some notes about Okonkwo as he is seen from two viewpoints: Ezinma's and Nwoye's.

Ezinma's view of Okonkwo:	Nwoye's view of Okonkwo:
character attributes:	character attributes:
incidents influencing her feelings:	incidents influencing his feelings:

Now write a short dialogue between Nwoye and Ezinma in which they discuss their father. Present your dialogue to the class.

3. Reverend Smith and Okonkwo share some characteristics. Write a comparison-and-contrast essay. Be sure to cite specific examples and details from the book.

Chapters 23-25, pp. 176-191

Summary: Okonkwo is briefly cheered by the burning of the church and the apparent solidarity among the clan members. His happiness turns to rage when he and five other leaders of Umuofia are imprisoned and mistreated until the clan's men raise the fine of 250 bags of cowries. When five court messengers appear to break up a meeting in the marketplace, Okonkwo draws his machete and beheads one of the messengers. Instead of joining the fight, the others disperse, and Okonkwo later hangs himself. According to tribal custom, he must be cut down and buried by strangers—the District Commissioner's men.

Vocabulary

palavers 193	unseemly 193	scuffle 194	sullen 194
pauper 195	sonorous 196	appease 197	vengeance 199
sacrilege 203	discerned 205	superfluous 206	pacification 209

Discussion Questions

1. Did Okonkwo and the other men who went to meet with the District Commissioner go there in good faith? *(They knew there could be trouble, but went with the idea of meeting as equals.)* How did the District Commissioner trick the Ibo men? *(He told them he wanted his men to listen to their grievances, but the men he brought in swiftly arrested the Ibo.)*

2. Did the court messengers follow the District Commissioner's orders regarding treatment of the men? *(No—the men were insulted and abused.)* Do you think the District Commissioner really knew how the men would be treated? Would they have been treated differently if they were Englishmen? Is this a genuine court—or is the District Commissioner acting more like a dictator?

3. In Chapter 23, what evidence do you find of dishonesty, greed, inhumanity and corruption? *(The District Commissioner lies to and tricks the Ibo men; the court messengers treat the men inhumanely and ask the villagers for an extra fifty bags of cowries, which are really for themselves.)* How do you think the District Commissioner and the court messengers would justify their actions?

4. How did the arrest of the leaders of Umuofia put the other villagers at a disadvantage? *(The people left to make decisions were not used to doing so.)*

5. Why do you think Achebe uses the phrase "he ground his teeth" three times on pages 200-201? *(perhaps to show how angry and determined Okonkwo is)* Why does Okonkwo think Egonwanne is a coward? *(Okonkwo thinks Egonwanne will tell the people not to fight a "war of blame" against the British.)*

6. At what point does Okonkwo know that the people will not go to war? *(When Okonkwo kills the court messenger, the people scatter and ask "Why did he do it?" If they were ready for war, they would not have asked why, but would have killed the other messengers.)*

7. How do you think the District Commissioner would react if presented with the concept of the Ibo as unique human beings, "different but equal"? *(He sees the Ibo as interesting inhabitants of the land—as he might view elephants or lions.)*

8. Could Okonkwo have made any choices other than these last two decisive ones—to take the messenger's life, then his own? What if he had done the first but not the second? the second but not the first?

9. What stories do you imagine were told about Okonkwo in the years which followed? Would you consider his final acts those of a fool or those of a brave hero fighting to defend his peoples' way of life? How do you think Achebe intended for you to see Okonkwo?

10. Should the clan have made allowances for unusual circumstances and buried Okonkwo "with full honors"—or would this in itself have been an insult to Okonkwo?

Supplementary Activities

Writing Activities

Write one of the following:
1. Ezinma's or Obierika's memorial poem for Okonkwo
2. The District Commissioner's report to his superiors regarding the death of the court messenger
3. The "reasonable paragraph" about Okonkwo that the District Commissioner puts in his book
4. A portion of the sermon Reverend Smith delivers to his flock the Sunday after Okonkwo kills the messenger and hangs himself

Post-reading Questions
for Discussion or Writing

1. Many critics see this book as an indictment of the Christian missionaries. What do you think? Were they simply sent ahead to split up clans and make it easy for an imperialistic government to take control? Or were they truly trying to save people they saw as "lost souls"?

2. Beginning in the late 1800s, Native American children were taken from reservations to Indian boarding schools, where they were taught the Christian religion and forbidden to speak their native languages. How is this situation similar to that in *Things Fall Apart?*

3. How does Achebe treat the theme of exploitation? What are some examples of exploitation in your world today? What are some characteristics of people and things which are often used for unprincipled gain by others? What motivates exploiters? How are the country and people of Nigeria being exploited today?

4. Were colonization and economic "progress" inevitable—or could life in Umuofia have remained as it had always been if things had happened differently? What could the Umuofians have done to preserve their way of life?

5. The British who colonized Nigeria described the native people as "primitive," "uncivilized," and "heathen"—all negative descriptors implying that a change "for the better" was necessary. How do their perceptions of the Africans show a limited point of view? How might Okonkwo have described the British way of life if he had gone to London?

6. Mr. Brown was respected by most members of the clan, while Reverend Smith was either despised or held in awe. How did the different attitudes of the two men influence the way they were received and treated? Which one do you consider a "thinking man"? Which is a "man of action"?

7. What themes are evident in *Things Fall Apart?*

8. To what extent do Okonkwo's character flaws cause his problems? What part is played by coincidence? How do external factors and forces—including those from his past—affect Okonkwo's life?

9. List some of the problems Okonkwo faced. What were his solutions? Rate his solutions on a scale of 1–5, with 1 being "very foolish" and 5 being "very wise." On average, where does he end up on the scale?

10. Give some reasons why this novel should or should not remain in your school's curriculum.

Post-reading Extension Activities

Writing Activities

Expository

1. Compare Okonkwo's character and life to that of Geronimo or Crazy Horse.

2. Consider Conrad's *Heart of Darkness.* Compare the impressions of Africa evoked by Conrad with those you got as you read Achebe's novel.

3. There are a number of warnings in the novel that the old way of life in Okonkwo's community is gradually deteriorating. Identify several points in the novel where Achebe foreshadows change.

4. Choose one of the following topics. What does Achebe have to say about it? Cite some examples from the novel.

ambition	*pride*	*greed*	*good and evil*
change	*betrayal*	*despair*	*family relationships*
race relations	*culture conflict*	*religion*	*tradition*

5. Choose three proverbs from the novel and explain the "deeper meaning" of each, that is, how it applies to the specific situation in the story. Find at least one other proverb which could have been included in the story. Explain why.

6. Explain and defend the actions of Okonkwo's fellow clansmen near the end of the novel, when they did not follow Okonkwo's lead and kill the other messengers. (If you like, do this in script form. Those who fled the scene talk later, affirming that they made the correct decision.)

7. Consider the position of women in Umuofian society. Were they in a subordinate or complementary position to men? Think about the significance of the woman with one leg, of the priestess Chielo, and of the bride-price. How did their place in the community at the beginning of the novel probably compare with the place the missionaries would advise for them later on?

8. Compare and contrast one of the following pairs of characters: Okonkwo and Nwoye; Okonkwo and Obierika; Mr. Brown and Reverend Smith; Ekwefi and Ezinma; Okonkwo and Reverend Smith.

9. Imagine a scenario in which the Ibo received fair trials. Prepare a closing statement to be presented by an attorney representing either (a) the men who burned down the church or (b) Okonkwo after he killed the court messenger. What will be the basis of defense for the actions of the defendant(s)?

10. Cite and describe the character traits you admire in Okonkwo and those you find undesirable. For each trait, explain why you feel as you do.

11. Did Okonkwo make the right choice when he beheaded the court messenger? Give three or more significant reasons why he should or should not have taken this action.

12. One reason Achebe wrote *Things Fall Apart* was to correct the misconceptions about Africa that were the result of books written by Europeans. He was particularly dismayed by Joyce Cary's *Mister Johnson* and by Joseph Conrad's *Heart of Darkness*. Think about some stereotypes you may have accepted about Africa before reading *Things Fall Apart*. Identify your own misconceptions, and explain how Achebe helped you to change your point of view.

13. How would Okonkwo define "success"? Compare and contrast his definition with your own. In what ways are your hopes and dreams similar? In what ways are they different?

14. Transfer Okonkwo's character traits to one of the following present-day people. What actions—whether you consider them "right" or "wrong"—would a person with Okonkwo's traits be most likely to take?
    (a) a farmer whose land and home are being bought by the state, against the farmer's wishes, in order to build a superhighway;
    (b) an environmentalist opposing the cutting of old-growth forest in the Northwest;
    (c) an animal-rights activist attending a pharmaceutical convention.

15. Read William Butler Yeats' poem, "The Second Coming" in its entirety. (It is found in many English literature anthologies.) Analyze the poem as it applies to the novel. In what ways is Achebe's novel an "answer" to Yeats' poem?

16. Achebe is a master of irony. Identify and explain some examples of irony found in *Things Fall Apart*.

Creative/Analytical
1. Using *The Iliad, The Odyssey,* or *Beowulf* as a model of the epic form, summarize Okonkwo's life in a poem of several pages. Include what you know about his early life and briefly allude to his various heroic accomplishments and his accumulation of wealth and attainment of success. Also include short descriptions of the mistakes he made.

2. Imagine that Ekwefi, Nwoye, or Ezinma has been keeping a diary. Write several of the most significant entries.

3. An **interior monologue** reveals a character's innermost thoughts. Write an interior monologue for Okonkwo after one of the following events: (a) the murder of Ikemefuna; (b) Chielo's trip to the oracle with Ezinma; (c) Okonkwo's arrival in Mbanta; (d) Okonkwo's release from the white man's prison.

4. You are Nwoye. You have just joined the missionary church. Write a persuasive letter to your mother and sisters telling them how happy you are and urging them to join you.

5. Write a chapter-length sequel to *Things Fall Apart,* set in Umuofia a few years after Okonkwo's death. Include a conversation in which several characters reminisce about Okonkwo. You may want to include a proverb or two as well.

6. Write the letter of condolence sent to Ikemefuna's mother by Ekwefi after the boy's death.

7. Write a eulogy for Okonkwo—a speech you would make at his funeral, if he had been able to have one.

8. When someone dies, family members and friends are comforted by happy memories of times they spent with the departed. What special memories of Okonkwo will be treasured by Ekwefi, Ezinma, and Obierika? (To complete this assignment, assume the persona of each character, and describe the memory in first person.)

9. Find a song that applies to the main problem in the novel (e.g., Bob Dylan's "The Times They Are A-Changin'"). Copy the words to the song you choose, and write an explanation of the connection between the song and the novel. Play the song for classmates and summarize your written explanation.

10. Write titles for each chapter.

Listening and Speaking

1. Read aloud some selections from one of Achebe's volumes of poetry. Discuss the poems. Look for themes and ideas similar to those found in *Things Fall Apart.*

2. Drums played an important part in the lives of Umuofians, broadcasting the news about births, deaths, feasts and festivities. Listed below are some African stories in which drums play a part. Have students work in groups, each with one story, to work out some rhythmic patterns (on desktops, cans with plastic lids, or real drums) to accompany the reading of their story. (The rhythms should *complement,* not drown out, the reading!)

Appiah, Peggy. *Ananse the Spider: Tales from an Ashanti Village.* New York: Pantheon, 1966.

Courlander, Harold. *The King's Drum and Other African Stories.* New York: Harcourt Brace, 1962.

Fuja, Abayomi. *Fourteen Hundred Cowries and Other African Tales.* New York: Lothrop, Lee and Shepard, 1971.

Rockwell, Anne. *When the Drum Sang: An African Folktale.* New York: Parent's, 1970.

Drama

1. Work with a group to create Okonkwo's story as a segment on a television documentary like "60 Minutes" or "20-20." The journalists should go "on location" to Umuofia to get both sides of the story, interviewing Okonkwo's friends and family, Reverend Smith, the District Commissioner, and anyone else you can fit into your script. Videotape your segment for presentation to your class.

2. Dramatize one of these important scenes:
   (a) After Ogbuefi Ezeudu warns Okonkwo not to take part in the murder of Ikemefuna, Okonkwo does so anyway.
   (b) Obierika and relatives of his daughter's suitor arrange Akueke's bride-price.
   (c) At Ezeudu's funeral, Okonkwo accidentally kills Ezeudu's son and must leave Umuofia immediately.
   (d) At the feast given before Okonkwo's departure from Mbanta, the eldest clan member warns of things to come.
   (e) Umuofian leaders meet with the District Commissioner, but are thrown into prison.

Language Study

1. When African slaves were brought to America, they brought their own languages with them. Many African-language words were assimilated into the uniquely American language. "Tote" comes from *tota;* "dig" in the sense of "understand," from *dega;* "hip" in the sense of "aware" from *hipi;* and "OK" from *yaw kay.* Do some research and find out what other words were brought from Africa.

Art

1. Create a calendar with sketches of important events in either (a) the novel or (b) village life in Umuofia.

2. Design postcards Ezinma might have sent from Mbanta to her friends back in Umuofia. Be sure to include messages.

3. Cut out, draw or photocopy pictures you think look like the characters in the novel. Make a poster showing Okonkwo in the middle and his friends and family around him. Include a brief descriptive caption for each character. For example, for Unoka you might write "Okonkwo's father: his failure kept Okonkwo striving for success." (You may be able to print out some photos from Internet sources or electronic encyclopedias.)

Music

1. Highlife, Juju, and Izzidi are types of music which are popular in Nigeria today. Find out more about popular Nigerian musicians Fela Anikulapu Kuti, Sonny Okosuns, King Sunny Ade, and I.K. Diaro. Some of their albums have been released internationally, so you may be able to listen to their music.

2. Sade Adu is a Nigerian whose music has become very popular in the United States. Listen to some songs by Sade and write a "review" for a jazz music magazine.

3. United States Rock and South Africa Jive got together for Paul Simon's album, *Graceland,* with help from the Soweto trio composed of Chikapa Phiri, Isaac Mthsli, and Baghiti Khumalo. Listen to the album. Then use the Reader's Guide to Periodical Literature to find out how the critics reacted when *Graceland* was first released. Summarize the critics' views and then give your own.

Social Studies/Current Events

1. Research what has happened politically in Nigeria since the British colonization. Construct a timeline showing major events.

2. Read an underground Nigerian newspaper, *Ochum's Revolutionary Times,* online at the website for the Coalition Against Dictatorship In Nigeria:

   http://www.sccs.swarthmore.edu/org/nigeria/index.html

Further Reading

Angelou, Maya. *All God's Children Need Traveling Shoes.* Random House, 1986. (recounts her experiences while living in Ghana)

Ba, Mariama. *So Long a Letter.* Heinemann, 1981. (the story of a Senegalese woman who is discarded by her husband)

Drew, Eileen. *Blue Taxis: Stories About Africa.* Milkweed Editions, 1989.

Emecheta, Buchi. *Bride Price.* Braziller, 1976. (a tragedy about love and rebellion in 1950s Nigeria)

Hudson, Mark. *Our Grandmother's Drums.* Henry Holt, 1991.

Soyinka, Wole. *Aké: The Years of Childhood.* Random House, 1981.

Just-for-Fun
Viewing

The Gods Must Be Crazy. If you have time for a "treat," this film by South African filmmaker Jamie Uys is both hilarious and poignant. Students will readily see some of Okonkwo's traits in the Bushman who is selected to rid his tribe of an evil thing sent by the gods—a Coke bottle.

Assessment for *Things Fall Apart*

Assessment is an on-going process, more than a quiz at the end of the book. Points for each project successfully completed may be placed in the "Teacher" column on the list below to show the level of achievement. Students should check off items as they complete them.

Name _____   Date_____

Student   Teacher

_____   _____   1.   As you read, keep a Response Journal. (See page 5 for some suggestions.)

_____   _____   2.   Analyze some of the proverbs found in the novel. Write about how a proverb applies to your life (page 12 of this guide).

_____   _____   3.   Participate in a classroom debate about one of the statements in Initiating Activity #1, page 5.

_____   _____   4.   Rewrite a scene in first person, from the point of view of one of the characters (page 15 of this guide).

_____   _____   5.   Research African folktales and re-tell one to your class.

_____   _____   6.   Write an essay helping someone with different beliefs to see your side of an issue.

_____   _____   7.   Dramatize a scene from the novel.

_____   _____   8.   Write a memorial poem for Okonkwo.

_____   _____   9.   After reading the novel, write an essay using one of the topics on pages 31-33 of this guide.

_____   _____   10.   Write a self-assessment about your study of this novel.

Note: For quizzes, tests, a study guide, and activity sheets focusing on critical thinking skills, vocabulary study, literary analysis, and writing skills, see the **Novel Units Student Packet** for *Things Fall Apart.*